Management of Motivation
and
Its Theories

B Hiriyappa

CONTENTS OF THE BOOK

Chapter No	Contents of the Chapter	Page No
1	**Introduction To Motivation** Introduction Meaning Of Motivation Nature And Characteristics Of Motivation Why Is Motivation Important? Motivation In Organizations	1 to 7
2	**Determinants Of Motivation** Introduction Definition Of Work Motivation And Challenges Dimensions Of Motivation Managerial Applications In Work Motivation Ways To Motivate People	8 to 15
3	**Five Concepts In Work Motivation** Introduction Managerial Issues And Work Challenges In Motivation Benefits Of Motivation	16 to 20
4	**Motivation And Rewards** Introduction Extrinsic Rewards Intrinsic Rewards	21 to 23
5	**Theories Of Motivation** Assumptions Of Motivation Theories Three Types Of Motivation Theory Major Theories Of Motivation	24 to 44

	Maslow's Need - Hierarchy Theory Of Motivation	
	Douglas McGregor Theory X And Theory Y	
	Comparison Of Theory X And Theory Y	
	Herzberg's Theory Of Motivation	
	Victor Vroom's Expectancy Theory	
	Mcclelland's Need For Achievement Theory	
	Essentials Of A Sound Motivational System	

CHAPTER 1
INTRODUCTION TO
MOTIVATION

Motivation According to Michael J. Juicus

"The act of stimulating someone or oneself to get a desired course of action"

Motivation According to Lewis Allen

"Motivation is the work a manager performs to inspire, encourage and impel people to take required action".

Motivation According to Dubin

"Motivation is the complex of forces starting and keeping a person at work in an organization. To put it generally, motivation starts and maintains an activity along a prescribed line. Motivation is something that moves the person to action, and continuous him in the course of action already initiated".

Motivation According to William G. Scott

"Motivation means a process of stimulating people to action to accomplish desired goals".

Motivation According to Koontz and O' Donnell

"Motivation is a general term applying to the entire class of drives, needs, wishes and similar forces".

Motivation According to Brch
"Motivation is a general inspiration process which gets the members of the team to pull their weight effectively, to give their loyalty to the group, to carry out properly the tasks they have accepted and generally to play an effective plan in the part in the job that the group has undertaken".

Motivation According to Dalton E. McFarland
"Motivation refers to the way in which urges, drives, desires, aspirations, striving or needs direct, control or explain the behavior of human beings".

Motivation According to Stephen P Robbins
"Motivation represents an unsatisfied need, which creates a state of tension, or disequilibrium, causing the individual to move in a goal directed pattern towards restoring a state of equilibrium by satisfying the need".

Motivation According to Tolman
"The term motivation has been called an intervening variable. Intervening variables are internal and psychological process which are not directly observable and which, in turn, account for behavior".

Motivation According to the Encyclopedia of Management
"Motivation refers to the degree of readiness of an organism to pursue some designated goal, and implies the

determination of the nature and locus of the forces, including the degree of readiness".

Motivation According to Mamoria

"Motivation is a willingness to expand energy to achieve a goal or reward. It is a force that activates dormant energies and sets in motion the action of the people. It is the function that kindles a burning passion for action among the human beings of an organization".

INTRODUCTION

"Interested people have to perform at a high level in a company; top level performance comes only from a highly motivated workforce". Business leader creates healthy environment: its influence to employee committed to work and gain superior performance and achieve superior goals. Employee happiness is directly linked to motivation, Motivation involves a constellation of closely related beliefs, perceptions, values, interests, and actions. Motivation within individuals tends to vary across subject areas, and this domain specificity increases with age.

MEANING OF MOTIVATION

Motivation is a state of mind and spirit of individual persons. High motivation leads to higher morale and greater production. A motivated employee gives his best to the organization. He stays loyal and committed to the organization. There is a different opinion about the terms of motivation. It can be applied as per the situation and time when it's applicable either negative or positive.

- ❖ The term motivation is derived from the Latin word "movere" which means - to move Forces "acting either on or   within a person to initiate behavior".

- ❖ Motivation is the term used to describe the forces within the individual that account for the level, direction, and persistence of effort expended at work.

- ❖ It is an incentive in terms of monetary and non monetary benefits of individual or group.

- ❖ It is the drive that makes you act in   a certain way to human beings in an organization.

- ❖ Motivation is a psychological process that causes the arousal, direction, and persistence of voluntary actions that are goal directed towards the achievement of the team work and goals of an enterprise.

- ❖ It is the willingness to exert high levels of effort to reach organizational goals, and it conditioned by the effort's ability to satisfy some individual need.

- ❖ Motivation can grow, leave or   change an individual or group.

- ❖ It refers to desire to accomplish a goal or participate in an endeavor.

- ❖ It refers to feelings that drive someone toward a particular objective.

- ❖ It refers to the need or desire that determines an individual's effort, behaviors and actions into planned work and non planned work.

❖ It refers to the forces either internal or external to a person that arouse enthusiasm and persistence to pursue a certain course of action within the specific time.

❖ Motivation is multifaceted.

❖ Middle level and low level People are motivated from the monetary incentives and top level people are motivated from the non monetary benefits.

❖ It influences to individual strive the amount of effort that an individual puts into doing something to achieve in a planned and organized manner.

❖ Motivation is the process of arousing and sustaining goal-directed towards the behavior.

❖ Motivation is the term used to describe the forces within the individual that account for the level, direction, and persistence of effort expended at work.

NATURE AND CHARACTERISTICS OF MOTIVATION

Motivating is the work of a manager in an organization to perform to inspire, encourage and impel people to take required action. The process of motivation is characterized in the following way:

Motivation Is an Internal Felling

❖ Motivation is a psychological phenomenon which generates in the mind of an individual feeling that he or she lacks certain things and needs those things.

- ❖ Motivation is a valuable force within an individual in an organization that drives him to behave in a certain way.

Motivation Is Related To Needs

- ❖ Needs are deficiencies which are created whenever there is physiological or psychological imbalance.

- ❖ In order to motivate people, we shall understand his/ her needs that call for satisfaction.

Motivation Produces Goal Oriented Behavior

- ❖ Goals are anything which will alleviate a need that reduces a drive.

- ❖ An individual's behavior is directed towards a attainment of goals.

Motivation Can Be Either Positive Or Negative

- ❖ Positive and negative motivation based on incentives or reward system in an organization.

- ❖ According to Flippo "positive motivation is a process of attempting to influence others to do your will through the possibility of gain or reward".

- ❖ Negative or fear motivation based on force or fear of an individual.

- ❖ Fear causes persons to act in a certain way due to they are afraid of the result if they don't want result in a task.

- ❖ Positive motivation like praise and credit for work done, wages and salaries, appreciation and delegation of authority and responsibility.

WHY IS MOTIVATION IMPORTANT?

Motivation is so important due to the following reasons are outlined:

- ❖ Under optimal conditions, effort can often be increased and sustained, it depends on change, stress and time of individual and group.

- ❖ Delegation without constant supervision is always necessary to maintain consistency in work area.

- ❖ Employees can become self-motivated to perform their duties and responsibilities that are assigned by the top management.

- ❖ Motivated employees can provide competitive advantage by offering suggestions & working to satisfy customers and clients.

MOTIVATION IN ORGANIZATIONS

Is it necessary motivation in organizations? It is necessary to Each employee who is working under business enterprise.

- ❖ To provide and maintain high Quality circles or employee involvement programs that are forms of participative management and are good ways to get people must involve in an organization.

- ❖ An organization shall introduce Variable pay programs as listed below:

  - Piece work plans.

  - Commission sales.

  - Gain-sharing programs.

  - Profit-sharing programs.

CHAPTER 2

DETERMINANTS OF MOTIVATION

INTRODUCTION

Motivation leads to accomplishment of short term and long term goals of an enterprise. Proper, appropriate motivation will be given to the right people at the right time to lead the mission and vision of an enterprise. Major determinants of motivation are Expectancy, Valence and other determinants like skills, abilities, role and opportunities in an organization.

Expectancy

It refers to The belief that one's efforts will positively influence one's performance. It is closely associated with individual job satisfaction and job enrichment.

It links with an individual's beliefs regarding the likelihood which being rewarded in accordance with his or her own level of performance in an organization.

Valence

It refers to the value a person lace on the rewards, he or she expects to receive from an organization. It's most important to the person to grow, develop and learn, improve performance and attitude in an enterprise.

Other Determinants

Other determinants are motivated to people are listed below:

- ❖ Skills and abilities,

- ❖ Role perceptions,

- ❖ Opportunities to perform

DEFINITION OF WORK MOTIVATION AND CHALLENGES

When we or he or she will take challenges, work stress, appropriate plan, organized work and proper motives that lead to highly positive outcome to either individual or an organization. Work motivation is a set of energetic forces that originate both within as well as beyond an individual's being, to initiate work-related behavior, and to determine its form, direction, intensity, and duration

Dimensions of Work Motivation

Directions, Intensity, Persistence are closely associated with Motivation. It depends on the following factors:

- ❖ Human Relations

- ❖ Vision

- ❖ Personality

Motivation produces motivation to work for developing a framework of motivational strategies that can apply in an organization in the following manner:

- ❖ It's helpful in planning and selecting instructional strategies in organizational elements like a human being and its work nature.

- ❖ It's helpful in tasks and activities for you and your employees during work time.

- ❖ It determines the ways that individual evaluate employee in the organization and apply recognition in terms of monetary and non monetary benefits.

DIMENSIONS OF MOTIVATION

There are four dimensions of motivation:

- ❖ Interest

- ❖ Relevance

- ❖ Expectancy

- ❖ Satisfaction

These dimensions are very useful to determine the following issues in an organization:

Planning for work motivation in the following issues directly relating to major and minor challenges that are applicable to the entity:

- ❖ Develop a comprehensive approach towards motivation.

❖ Ready to adjust motivational strategies to your instructional situation in an organization.

❖ Build motivational issues into all levels of your instructional planning in an organization.

❖ Capture employee interest in the subject matter and nature of workforce in an organization.

❖ Highlight the relevance of the subject matter and work culture in an organization to identify needs and demand require from industry.

❖ Vary individual instructional strategies throughout the instructional lesson to maintain interest in the best interest of the job and its performance to achieve to lead role.

❖ Effectively plan for active work involvement in an organization and encourage employees in work participation.

❖ Better to select strategies that capture appropriate work curiosity.

❖ Better to select strategies & present training and development material with the appropriate degree of challenge & difficulty in work position.

❖ Proper design role of group employees for specific tasks.

❖ Design the work design to promote an employee into success form

❖ Allow an employee to control work and curb uncontrollable tasks in the job.

- ❖ An individual expresses interest in the content & project enthusiasm in an organization and try to accept suggestions and instructions from an employee.

- ❖ Provide opportunities to learn and earn and promote to positions.

- ❖ Try to support workers' attempts to understand their challenges.

- ❖ Motivational Strategies Concerning Evaluation & Feedback work issues are as follows:

    o Establish evaluation expectations & criteria for assessment of employee performance.

    o Selection procedures for monitoring & judging employees nature of work.

    o Decide when to give feedback & rewards towards employees.

    o Select the types of feedback & rewards to each employee in an organization.

    o Help employee to feel satisfied with their learning, training and its outcomes.

    o Use mistakes & redoing work as learning opportunities in this way to overcome employee mistakes.

    o Press employees to think about their job and its outcome.

MANAGERIAL APPLICATIONS IN WORK MOTIVATION

It is very difficult to apply managerial applications in work motivation. When it defines clearly managerial application in an enterprise than it manageable and acceptable the outcome.

❖ It clarifies people's expectancies that their effort will lead to performance in an organization.

❖ Administer rewards that are positively valuable to employees in an organization.

❖ It is clearly linked to value rewards and performance of an employee.

❖ One important functions of management are to motivate staff for following reasons:

   o Job performance (ability)

   o Productivity (skills)

   o Job satisfaction

   o Employee extension

Motivation Through Job Design In An Organization

There are Five Core Dimensions of Work for job design in an organization as listed below:

Skill Variety

❖ It refers to the variety of activities required in carrying out the work.

Task identity

- ❖ It refers to the completion of a "whole" and identifiable piece of work.

Task Significance

- ❖ It determines how substantial an impact the job has on the lives of other people.

Autonomy

It involves the freedom, independence, and discretion that one has to do the job.

Job Feedback

It determines how much performance feedback the job is provided to the worker.

WAYS TO MOTIVATE PEOPLE

- ❖ Motivation plays vital role for motivating to people in the following ways:

- ❖ Training

- ❖ Coaching

- ❖ Task assignments

- ❖ Rewards contingent on good performance

- ❖ Valued rewards available

- ❖ Suitable punishment for effective feedback and reengineering process than provide positive incentives to such employee

- ❖ Promotion.

- ❖ Develop an alternative motivation plan when will get negative feedback and performance of an employee, it is suitable to make converts negative into positive feedback.

CHAPTER 3

FIVE CONCEPTS IN WORK MOTIVATION

INTRODUCTION

There are five concepts in work motivation which influence job design and job enrichment in an organization. Five concepts in work motivation as listed below:

Behavior

- ❖ It refers to the action from which we or she or he infer motivation; it is one of the important concepts in work motivation.

- ❖ Study of individual behavior, it plays a vital role in the determination of work motivation in the organization.

Performance

- ❖ It refers to evaluation of behavior an individual in an organization.

❖ A performance that determining the monetary and non monetary reward to individuals in an organization.

❖ It's based on the ability and standard roles and responsibility towards an organization.

Ability

❖ It refers to the determinant of the behavior of an individual in an organization.

❖ It is able to determine that an individual is able to work in different work environments and in this way achievement of tasks and goals which are specified in an organization.

Situational Constraints

❖ It refers to determinant of behavior in organizations.

❖ Situational constraints are very important to understand the different types of behavior obtained from different situation

❖ It is also very essential to evaluate motivational factors in terms of monetary and non monetary benefits to an employee in an organization.

Motivation

❖ It is a determinant of behavior in an organization, group, and individual personal operation.

❖ It is the force of the individual person who will put risk and also good salary

MANAGERIAL ISSUES AND WORK CHALLENGES IN MOTIVATION / BENEFITS OF MOTIVATION

The manager's primary task is to motivate others to perform the tasks efficiently and effectively in an organization. It is one of the challenges in an organization. Managers must find the major keys to manage and guide, supervise of subordinates to come to work regularly and on time, to work hard, and to make positive contributions towards the effective and efficient achievement of organizational objectives. Motivation is effective instruments in the hands of a manager for inspiring the workforce and creating confidence in it. Managers motivating the work force in management and creates 'will to work' which is necessary for the achievement of organizational goals. The various managerial issues and work challenges in motivation are listed below:

- ❖ Motivation is one of the important elements in the directing process in organizations. Managers are motivating the workers manage the workers and director guides the workers' and their actions for the desired result of accomplishing the major tasks of the organization.

- ❖ Working will tend to be as efficient as possible by improving upon their skills and knowledge so that they are able to contribute to the progress of the organization thereby increasing productivity. There fore, it is a key focus area in an organization.

❖ Mangers will bring organizational effectiveness, it becomes to degree a question about the management and its ability to motivate its employees for this purpose to direct at least a reasonable effort towards the goals of the organization.

❖ Effective motivation contributes to good industrial relations in the organization; this is only possible only when the workers are motivated, contented and disciplined. If the frictions between the workers and the management the motivation skills will be reduced conflicts between workers and management.

❖ Motivation is the best remedy for resistance to changes in an organization. If the changes are introduced in an organization, it will be created resistance from the workers and management. But if the workers of an organization are motivated this circumstance they will accept, introduce and implement the changes whole heartily and help to keep the organization on the right track of progress.

❖ Motivation facilities like incentives and morale to the maximum utilization of all factors of production human, physical and financial resources and thereby contributes to higher production in this way achieved to maximum growth and development of an organization.

❖ Motivation promotes a sense of belonging among the workers in an organization that creates a good feel to workers about the performance of enterprise and interest of the enterprise.

❖ Many organizations are now beginning to pay increasing attention to developing their employees as future resources as assets in an organization which can draw as they grow and develop in an organization.

CHAPTER 4

MOTIVATION AND REWARDS

INTRODUCTION

Motivation and rewards influence to Employee to must commit with project of an enterprise and complete within stipulated time. The employee always expects a high degree of motivation and rewards for their work and its completion of the task. It enhances and enriched the job satisfaction and job enrichment. A reward is a workable outcome of positive value to the individual that is provided by an organization. There are two types of reward as illustrated in exhibit 4.1:

Exhibit – 4.1: Types of Reward

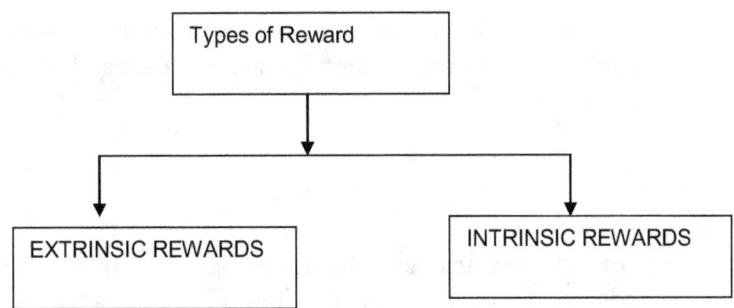

Extrinsic Rewards

- ❖ Extrinsic rewards are those rewards which are externally administered for example pay and verbal praise; the motivational stimulus originates outside the person.

- ❖ Extrinsic rewards are given by another person.

- ❖ Payoffs (external) granted to the individual by others in the form of money, employee benefits, promotions, recognition, status symbols and praise.

Improving Performance with Extrinsic Rewards

- ❖ Rewards must satisfy individual needs in the form of cafeteria compensation: it is a plan that allows employees to select their own mix of benefits getting from an organization.

- ❖ Employees must believe that effort will lead to an attainable reward in an organization.

- ❖ Rewards must be personally and socially equitable in an organization.

- ❖ Rewards must be linked to performance (results) such that desired behaviors are encouraged in an organization.

Intrinsic Rewards

- ❖ Intrinsic rewards are those rewards which are self-administered; they occur "naturally" as a person performs a task.

❖ The feelings of competency, personal development, and self-control people experience in their work.

❖ An intrinsic reward is satisfactions a person receives in the process of performing a particular action.

❖ Self-granted and internally experienced payoffs   in the form of Sense of accomplishment, self-esteem, and self-actualization

Both Intrinsic and Extrinsic rewards can help the manager to lead effectively through motivation, and to achieve maximum motivational impact, it is necessary to effectively identify with   performance and way of determining of rewards for this purpose we shall consider the following issues:

❖ Respect diversity and individual differences in an organization

❖ A manager can clearly understand what people want from work in an organization.

❖ Proper Allocate rewards to an employee in an organization in this way satisfy the interests of both individuals and the organization.

CHAPTER 5
THEORIES OF MOTIVATION

INTRODUCTION
Business leaders must understand the different motivation theories and its application in business enterprise. An organization consists of group employees who are coming different background and culture. Therefore, team leader or manager or team member knows the various theories of motivation and useful. When he or she know the theories of motivation: its outcome is effective application and proper management of motivation in an organization.

ASSUMPTIONS OF MOTIVATION THEORIES
A manager or business leader knows the basic assumptions of motivation theories and major assumptions which relate to motivation theories as outlined:

- ❖ The behavior has a starting point, a direction, and a stopping point

- ❖ The focus is on voluntary behavior under the control of the person

- ❖ Behavior is not random. It has purpose and direction

THREE TYPES   OF MOTIVATION THEORY

Content Theory

❖ It refers to needs which are physiological and psychological deficiencies that an individual feels some compulsion to eliminate.

Process Theory

❖ It refers to people who give meaning to rewards and the work opportunities available to them.

Reinforcement Theory

❖ It refers to people's whose behavior is influenced by its environmental and its consequences.

MAJOR THEORIES OF MOTIVATION

Motivation to work is very complex tool in an organization. There are many internal and external environmental variables which are affecting the motivation to work in an organization. Behavioral scientists started to search new facts and techniques for motivation. The most important theories are explained below:

I. Need Approaches / Content Theroy :

❖ Maslow's Hierarchy of Needs

❖ Alderfer's ERG Theory

❖ Herzberg's Two Factor Theory

❖ McClelland's Learned Needs Theory

II. Cognitive Approaches / Process Theory :

- ❖ Expectancy Theory

- ❖ Equity Theory/ Social Comparison

- ❖ Goal Setting Theory

III. Reinforcement Theory or Operant Conditioning

We shall discuss only important theories in motivation:

MASLOW'S NEED - HIERARCHY THEORY OF MOTIVATION

Dr. Abraham Maslow Developed this theory in 1940. Need Hierarchy theory Based on four major assumptions:

Four assumptions as outlined:

1. Only unmet needs motivate

2. People's needs are arranged in order of importance (basic – complex)

3. Lower-level needs must be met first

4. There are 5 classifications of need

Dr. Abraham Maslow developed a five-step process which describes man's behavior in terms of the needs he experiences. These needs are presented in the exhibit – 5.1:

- ❖ Maslow's theory of motivation that is based on five needs.

    - o These needs are arranged in order of importance.

o Each level must be at least minimally satisfied before the motivation to satisfy a higher level will occur. Needs are :

- Physiological needs

- Safety needs

- Social needs

- Esteem needs

- Self-actualization

Exhibit – 5.1: Maslow's Hierarch of Needs Theory

Fulfillment off the job	Need Hierarchy	Fulfillment on the job
Education, religion, hobbies, personal growth	Self Actualization Needs	Opportunities for training , growth and creativity
Approval of Family, Friends, community	Esteem Needs	Recognition, high status, increased responsibilities
Family, Friends, and community groups	Belongings needs	Work groups, clients, coworkers, supervisors
Freedom from war, pollution, violence	Safety needs	Safe work, fringe benefits, job security
Food, water, shelter	Physiological needs	Heat, air, base salary

Hierarchy of Needs

1. Physiological

❖ It refers to Primary or basic needs, i.e. air, food, shelter, sex and relief or avoidance of pain, Heat, and base salary.

2. Safety

   ❖ Once the physiological needs are met, the individual is concerned with safety and security.

   ❖ For example: Freedom from war, pollution, violence, Safe work, fringe benefits, job security.

3. Belongingness

   ❖ After safety needs, people look for love, friendship, acceptance, and affection.

   ❖ Example of Social Needs: Family, friends, community, groups Work groups, clients, coworkers and supervisors.

4. Esteem

   ❖ After social needs, the individual focuses on ego, status, self-respect, recognition for accomplishments and feeling of self-confidence and prestige

   ❖ For example: Approval of family, friends, Community, Recognition, high status and increased responsibilities

5. Self-Actualization

   ❖ It refers to Highest level of need is to develop one's full potential. To do so, one seeks growth, achievement, and advancement.

❖ For example: Education, religion, hobbies, personal growth, Opportunities for training, advancement, growth and creativity.

DOUGLAS MCGREGOR THEORY X AND THEORY Y

Theory X and Theory Y were developed by Douglas McGregor. He has classified the basic assumption regarding human nature into two parts and has designated them as 'theory X, and theory Y,

Theory X According to Douglas McGregor

The "Theory X" management theory holds that the average employee has little ambition, dislikes work *and* must be coerced, controlled *and* directed to achieve organizational objectives

Those in management who believe the behavioral assumption of "**Theory X**" take an **autocratic approach** to get work done

Theory X Assumptions

❖ Management is responsible for organizing the elements of productive enterprises like money, material, equipment; people are in the interest of economic ends.

❖ People do not like work and try to avoid it.

❖ Managers have to control, direct, coerce, and threaten employees to get them to work toward organizational goals.

* People prefer to be directed, to avoid responsibility, and to want security; they have little ambition.

* He lacks ambition, dislikes responsibility and prefers to be led.

* He is inherently self centered, indifferent to organizational needs.

* He is by nature resistant to change.

* He is gullible, not very bright.

Theory Y According to Douglas McGregor

The "Theory Y" management theory holds that the average employee does not dislike the work, *is* self-directed, *is* creative and imaginative, accepts responsibility *and* is committed to achieving organizational needs and objectives

"Theory Y" encourages managers to **support** and **encourage employees** in efforts to higher achievement.

Theory Y Assumptions

* People seek both seek responsibility and accept responsibility under favorable conditions.

* People can be innovative in solving problems.

* People are bright, but under most organizational conditions their potentials are underutilized.

* The work conditions are favorable and also an average human being does not inherently dislike work.

❖ Here, man can exercise self control and self direction in the services of objectives to which he is committed.

❖ Commitment to objectives is a result of the rewards associated with their achievement. People select a goal for themselves if they see the possibilities of some kind of reward that may be material or even psychological.

COMPARISON OF THEORY X AND THEORY Y

Table – 5.1: Comparison of Theory X and Theory Y

Theory X	Theory Y
It assumes human beings inherently dislike work and distasteful towards work.	It assumes that work is as natural as play or rest.
It emphasis that people do not have ambitions and they shirk responsibilities.	It is just the reverse.
It assumes that person's creativity.	It assumes to have little capacity for is widely distributed in the population creativity.
People lack self motivated and require to be externally controlled.	Theory Y people are creative.
It emphasizes upon the centralization of authority in the decision making process.	Theory Y emphasizes decentralization and greater participation.

HERZBERG'S THEORY OF MOTIVATION

Herzberg Two-Factor theory Developed in the 1960s. It's based on two levels of Needs are listed below:

1. Lower-level: Hygiene or Maintenance

2. Higher-level: Motivators

In this theory, People are motivated by motivators rather than by maintenance factors

Exhibit – 5.2: Herzberg's Two-Factor Theory

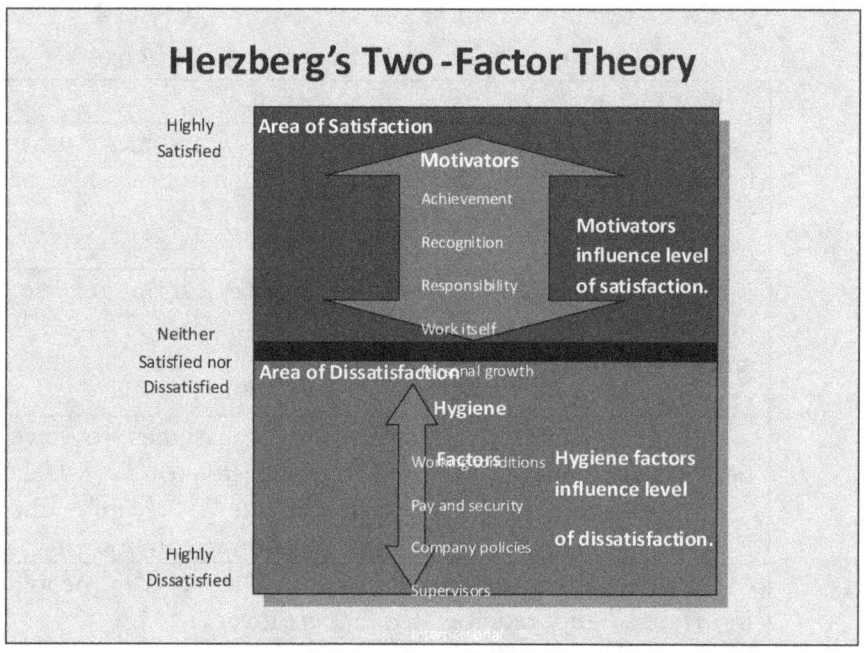

Herzberg's Theory Rests on Two Assumptions

1. Job satisfaction is equivalent to being motivated (influence of Human Relations) and assumption that the happy worker is a productive worker.

2. Job satisfaction and dissatisfaction are separate concepts with unique determinants.

Frederick Herzberg's "Motivation-Hygene Theory" - defined two independent categories of needs as listed below:

- ❖ Hygiene factors
- ❖ Motivators

Hygiene Factors/ Maintenance/ Extrinsic Factors

- ❖ It refers to salary, fringe benefits, security (Civil Service), rules and regulations and supervision.

- ❖ Motivation comes from outside the person and the job itself

- ❖ Include: pay, job security, title, working conditions, fringe benefits, and relationships

- ❖ All factors related to lower-level needs

Motivators / Intrinsic Factors

- ❖ It refers to challenging assignment, increased responsibility, recognition for work and individual growth.

- ❖ Motivation comes from within the person through the work itself.

- ❖ Include: achievement, recognition, challenge, and advancement.

❖ All factors related to higher-level needs.

Comparison of Herzberg's Two Factor Theory

Table – 5.2: Comparison of Herzberg's Two Factor Theory

Determinants of Job Dissatisfaction are **Hygiene** Factors:	Determinants of Job Satisfaction are **Motivating** Factors:
Pay, fringe benefits	Work itself, responsibility
Working conditions	Advancement
Quality of supervision	Recognition
Interpersonal relations	

Contributions of Herzberg theory

❖ First to argue that the job content/design job was important

❖ Job enrichment as a motivational strategy

❖ Model appealing, easy to understand

❖ Explained why "more" hygiene factors did not increase motivation

Criticisms of Herzberg theory

❖ Some individual   differences, like the desire to pay, rejected as a motivator. Not everyone wants an enriched job.

❖ Assumes satisfaction = motivation

❖ May be "method-bound" by self-serving bias

VICTOR VROOM'S EXPECTANCY THEORY

Expectancy theory was developed by Victor H. Vroom. It's based on the notion that human behavior depends on people's expectations concerning their ability to perform tasks and to receive desired rewards. This theory argues that the strength of a tendency to act in a certain way depends on the strength of an expectation that the act will be followed by a given outcome and on the attractiveness of the outcome to the individual.

Expectancy Theory Relating With the Following Issues In Expectancy Theory

❖ Motivation depends on individuals' expectations about their ability to perform tasks and receive desired rewards.

❖ It concerned not with identifying types of needs but with the thinking process that individuals use to achieve rewards.

❖ It's based on the effort, performance, and desirability of outcomes.

Basic Assumptions of the Expectancy theory

- ❖ Individuals decide their own behaviors in organizations

- ❖ Different individuals have different needs and goals, and want different rewards

- ❖ Individuals decide among alternatives based on their perceptions

Expectancy theory Variables

It includes three variables which Vroom refers as listed below:

Expectancy

Expectancy is a person's perception of the probability of accomplishing an objective. It refers to a person's belief that working hard will result in a desired level of task of performance.To Maximize Expectancy in the following ways:

- ❖ Select workers with ability

- ❖ Train workers to use an ability

- ❖ Support work effort

- ❖ Clarify performance goals

Instrumentality

It refers to a person's belief that successful task performance will be followed by rewards and other potential outcomes.

To Maximize Instrumentality in the following ways:

- ❖ Clarify psychological contracts

- ❖ Communicate performance-outcome possibilities

- ❖ Demonstrate what rewards are contingent on performance

Valence

- ❖ It refers to the value a person places on the outcome or reward

- ❖ The value a person assigns to possible rewards and other work-related outcomes.

To Maximize Valence in the following ways:

- ❖ ID needs and adjust rewards to match.

- ❖ Clearly define objectives and the necessary performance needed to achieve them.

- ❖ Tie performance to rewards.

- ❖ Be sure rewards are of value to the employee.

- ❖ Make sure your employees believe you will do as you

- ❖ Promise.

Vroom's formula: Motivation = Expectancy × Valence

Exhibit – 5.3: Vroom's Expectancy Theory

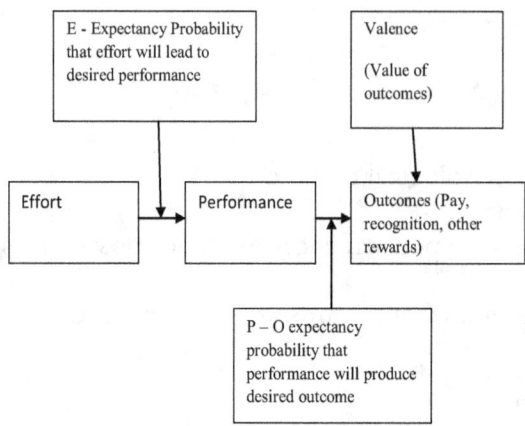

MCCLELLAND'S NEED FOR ACHIEVEMENT THEORY

David C. McClelland, a Harvard Psychologists developed in the 1940s. He has proposed that there are three major relevant motives most needs in workplace situations. According to him, the motives are listed below:

❖ The need for achievement i.e., strives to succeed

❖ The need for affiliation i.e., warm relationships with others

❖ The need for power i.e., control other people

The Need for Achievement

Important issues which are related to the need for achievement as listed below:

❖ A person wants to take personal responsibility for solving problems.

❖ It is based on Goal oriented; set moderate, realistic, attainable goals.

❖ A person seeks challenge, excellence, and individuality.

❖ A person Take calculated, moderate risk.

❖ A person Desire concrete feedback on their performance.

❖ A person willing to work hard.

❖ A person Tasks must be challenged with clear attainable objectives

❖ Fast and frequent feedback a must require by a person

❖ Continued increases in responsibility towards by individual person.

Need For Achievement And Behavior

Money is important to both high and low achievers, but for different reasons as below:

❖ High achiever wants concrete feedback about performance.

❖ Making a profit, or receiving a bonus, is a statement about success or failure.

❖ Symbol of success and feedback about job performance.

❖ High achiever wants a challenging job and responsibility for the work.

- ❖ Want to feel successful at doing something over which they have control.

- ❖ Low achiever views monetary reward as an end in itself.

- ❖ Get increased performance from low Need for Achievement person by rewarding with money.

- ❖ Managers and executives usually have a stronger Need for Achievement than people in other occupations.

- ❖ Evidence points to strong Need for Achievement as an entrepreneur characteristic.

- ❖ Nature of Need for Achievement behavior fits well with such role demands.

The Need for Affiliation

Strong **Need for Affiliation** people look for the following issues:

- ❖ Focuses on "establishing, maintaining, and restoring positive affective relations with others".

- ❖ An individual wants close, warm interpersonal relationships.

- ❖ An individual Seek the approval of others, especially those about whom they care.

- ❖ Like other people, want other people to like them, and want to be in the company of others.

- ❖ An individual seeks a close relationship with others.

- ❖ An individual wants to be liked by others.

- ❖ An individual enjoys lots of social activities.

- ❖ Seek to belong; join groups and organizations.

- ❖ Must work as part of a team.

- ❖ Satisfaction derived from the people, not the task.

- ❖ Needs lots of praise and recognition in organization.

- ❖ Delegate responsibility for training and orientation in the organization.

- ❖ Good buddies and/or mentors required in an organization.

The Need For Power

- ❖ Need to be able to plan and control.

- ❖ Inclusion in decision making necessary, especially when affected.

- ❖ Best performance along within them.

- ❖ Assign whole tasks, not parts

- ❖ Want to control the situation.

- ❖ Want to influence of control over others.

- ❖ Enjoy competition and winning; do not like to lose.

- ❖ Willing to confront others.

Relationship Between Need For Achievement And Need For Power

Some relationships are discussed below:

❖ Strong Need for Achievement person would be :

- Task centered

- Future oriented

- Performs to internal standard of excellence

❖ Strong Need for Power person would be :

- Draws attention

- Risk taking

- Present oriented

- Assesses situations for change potential

❖ Both types of people are important for successful survival of an organization.

❖ Strong Need for Achievement managers keep an organization going in well form in associated with power and affiliation.

❖ Strong Need for Power people bring dramatic change and innovation for change and development of an organization.

ESSENTIALS OF A SOUND MOTIVATIONAL SYSTEM

A careful comparison and integration of the above theories of motivation suggest the essential of a sound motivational system as outlined:

❖ It should be adopt a positive, purposeful a progressive view of man, i.e., it is capable of be molded to offer constructive co- operation to task requirement of an organization.

❖ It is able to recognize individual differences in terms of perceptions, values, needs and abilities as also their dynamic nature's role in the organization.

❖ It is able to relate the goals of the organization within the individual goals of participants.

❖ It will give due weightage to group dynamic, motivation is not a mere individual phenomenon but is very much influenced by interpersonal situations. Similarly, other environmental influences are also to be taken into consideration in a sound motivational system.

❖ It will incorporate aspects of training and development of people, sound leadership and supervision, wholesome working conditions, redesign of jobs to make them more meaningful and participation of people in processes of decision making and implementation.

❖ There should be an appropriate combination of monetary and non monetary incentives; also the structure of motivating factors should be equitably designed at different levels of the organization.

❖ The system will rule out manipulator devices to motivate people by such superficial gimmicks of socialization, paternalism and patronizing attitudes and so on towards people.

❖ There should be adequate and efficient mechanism for feedback on performance. People should be informed periodically on how they perform and how they can further improve their performance.

❖ Efforts should be made to monitor the attitudes and behavior of people; both as individuals and as members of the group.

❖ The linkages between abilities and efforts and performance efforts and rewards need to be clarified in unmistakable terms.

❖ There should be contingent provisions for penalty for persistently unacceptable performance and behavior on the part of some people.

www.ingramcontent.com/pod-product-compliance
Lightning Source LLC
Chambersburg PA
CBHW081232170526
45165CB00009B/3041